Kids

Hike. Contemplate what makes you happy and what makes you happier still. Follow a trail or blaze a new one. **Hike.** Think about what you can do to expand your life and someone else's. **Hike.** Slow down. Gear up. **Hike.** Connect with friends. Re-connect with nature.

Hike. Shed stress. Feel blessed. **Hike** to remember. **Hike** to forget. **Hike** for recovery. **Hike** for discovery. **Hike.** Enjoy the beauty of providence. **Hike.** Share the way, The Hiker's Way, on the long and winding trail we call life.

Hike
With
Kids

BY
JOHN MCKINNEY

TheTrailmaster.com

Acknowledgments: This author was assisted immeasurably in writing this book by hiking with the students and teachers at Santa Barbara Open Alternative School, The Waldorf School and Santa Barbara Middle School. I will always treasure those many miles of trail we hiked together. Thank you! And thanks Sophia and Daniel; you've grown-up on the trail in so many ways and Dad is very proud of you. A special thanks to our trail buddy, Huckleberry Hebert, and to the many friends who came hiking with me and their kids or entrusted their kids to me for a day on the trail; the most practical advice in this book comes from my time with kids because I learned as much from them as they from me.

Book Design by Lisa DeSpain
HIKE Series Editor: Cheri Rae

Published by: Olympus Press and The Trailmaster, Inc.

TheTrailmaster.com (Visit our site for a complete listing of all Trailmaster publications, products, and services)

To the kids in my life:
Sophia, Daniel, Rosemary and Luke

HIKE ON.

"You're off to great places, today is your day.
Your mountain is waiting, so get on your way."

—Dr. Seuss

CONTENTS

The family that plays (hikes!) together stays together.
Enjoy your special time on the trail.

Introduction

What's America's most popular form of outdoor recreation?

No, it's not soccer or fishing or biking.

It's hiking. And most adults who enjoy time on the trail got started as kids.

It's a gift from one generation to the next to take kids on a hike, but giving that gift is easier said than done. Hiking faces heavy competition for children's attention from other activities and from electronic games and digital devices. It's a challenge to get kids on the trail and there's a shortage of adults willing to take them.

But where there is a will there is a way. You supply the will, and I'll show you the way, the hiker's way.

HIKE With Kids aims to inspire adults to take kids hiking, and provide the practicalities to do so. You and the kids will have fun, you will teach them outdoors skills, and contribute to their good health. Kids gain improved social skills and school performance from time on the trail. Hiking leads to a lifetime commitment to conservation. And hiking in nature offers one of the best opportunities and environments for meaningful communication. We could all—adults and kids alike—use more of that these days.

A hike, by definition, is a walk in nature. Nature is the key element. All hikes are walks but not all walks are hikes.

I wrote *Hike with Kids* to help adults—parents, grandparents, relatives, teachers and youth leaders—do just that. You'll learn the many benefits hiking offers kids—from improved fitness and focus to mastering a rewarding activity to last a lifetime.

Hike with Kids will help you with the basics. You'll learn some easy ways to select hiking gear (and only the gear you really need), choose a hike that's just right for you and the kids in your charge, how to travel safely and have a great time in nature. You'll learn about the opportunities and challenges of hiking with each age group and how to maximize the experience.

I've been fortunate to take kids of all ages on hikes and learned a thing or two along the way. I've hiked with my son and daughter from infancy to young adulthood. I've hiked with school groups as well as with Scout and church groups.

For many years I wrote a weekly hiking column for the Los Angeles Times. When I started as a young, single guy, I wrote about all-day treks and high-altitude challenges; when I got married, I wrote about romantic beach strolls and exotic hiking vacations. Not until I became a father did I write much about nature walks and family-friendly trails and advise my readers about the best places to take a hike with kids.

One of the least-recognized advantages of hiking is that it is a lifetime sport: wherever you are in your life you can enjoy it and share the experience with others. Parenthood, as I, and millions more parents have discovered, is the most obvious stage in life to hike with kids—your own kids and their friends.

In addition, we have many more roles in this life: aunt, uncle, grandparent, sibling, service club volunteer and school field trip coordinator. In all of these roles and many more, we can find ourselves with the wonderful opportunity to take kids on a hike.

Seize that opportunity or make one. Help kids achieve that wonderful perspective on the natural world gained by walking through it at two or three miles per hour. Be a good listener and know that hearing a kid out in the great outdoors is one of the greatest gifts an older hiker can give a younger one.

As Mr. Rogers advises: "If adults can show what they love in front of kids, there'll be some child who says, 'I'd like to be like that!' or 'I'd like to do that!'"

Don't worry, adults. You can do it. Take the kids to the trailhead, take them by the hand, and take a hike.

Getting Back on the Nature Trail

Time spent in nature contributes to the health and wellbeing of children, their families, and their communities at large.

These days, though, time spent in nature is undervalued, and the price we pay for our estrangement from nature is much higher than we acknowledge.

I believe we can help affect a societal shift to a belief in the restorative power of nature. One step at a time. By hiking. Especially by hiking with children.

Getting youth into nature and teaching kids and teens hiking skills contributes to good health, improved social skills and school performance, and results in a lifetime commitment to conservation. We must extend the opportunity to take a hike to all children, from every race and cultural background and economic circumstance. We must leave no child behind. We must leave no child inside.

It's imperative we encourage and empower parents, family members, friends, teachers and youth leaders to share their hiking skills and love of nature with younger generations.

Our mission to connect/re-connect children and adults to the outdoors is time-critical, and we must act now to ensure present and future generations will enjoy, appreciate, and preserve our natural world as much and, hopefully more, than previous generations.

—Hike On.
John McKinney

The Trailmaster's Four Essentials for Hiking with Kids

Give them nature.

Give them nurture.

Hike smart.

Have fun.

HIKE ON.

It's time for those of us who believe in the
joys of hiking to lead children
back into nature.

1

Nature

These days, adults aren't the only ones feeling rushed, stressed, and unfulfilled. Our babies and toddlers spend their time in day-care; our school-aged children are way over-scheduled, and subjected to far more organized activities and more homework than were most of their parents, and our teens are on what some have called a "race to nowhere," with expectations of academic achievement crowding out all other activities, including family time.

Perhaps you've observed overbearing, overprotective parents who hover over their children, and encourage them to stay quietly inside on their scheduled play dates, instead of sending them outside to create their own fun. Formerly called "helicopter parents" and now called "lawnmower parents," they may be well intended but miss the point of letting children spend unstructured time outdoors. High-stress schools that demand hours in front of screens and confine children indoors—are taking the fun out of childhood and keeping kids from experiencing the natural world.

It's time for those of us who believe in the joys of hiking to lead children back into nature. We owe it to them to articulate an alternative vision of growing up in the "real" world—the natural world.

Leave No Child Inside!

Children need to get out the door and on the trail; and it's the job of caring adults to make that happen. In our obsession with intellectual achievement and academic testing, we forget about teaching the self-reliance that can be gained with repeated experience in the great classroom of the great outdoors.

When we take children hiking, we instill in them an experiential love of the earth that is very different from any lesson in school. For all our good intentions of educating children about The Environment, Saving the Planet and Going Green, far too many children know more about nature in the abstract than from first-hand experience. They study the tropical rainforest in Brazil, the plight of the polar bear and the fate of the whales, but what do they know about native plants, peaks, and creeks?

We teach them about recycling, the evils of pesticides and plastic, and the urgency of climate change.

They've watched hours and hours of video of massive oil spills, wildfires, hurricanes and floods. But what do we teach them of the natural world nearby?

In their worlds with too much time spent multitasking, sitting in traffic, eating fast food and worrying about homework, good grades and test results—not to mention the usual concerns about popularity, fitting in and figuring it all out, our kids need nature more than ever before. They need to get their feet on the ground, their minds clear and their vision extended all the way to the wide horizon. They need to breathe deep and inhale the heady fragrance of Mother Nature in all her glory.

It's time to step up efforts to make sure everyone is welcome to join the hiking community.

Inclusivity in the Great Outdoors

When we discuss the best ways to connect kids to nature, it's important to clarify that by kids we mean *all* kids, without regard to their color, culture, where they live or the economic circumstances of their families.

I have been pleased to note a shift on the part of park agencies and by hikers themselves toward a more inclusive vision. Many hiking and conservation organizations fully embrace the concept of equity, that is to say the idea that everyone, no matter where they live or how much money they make should have access to the natural world and the opportunity to take a hike. It's obvious to veteran hikers, there's a greater diversity of trail users now than ever before.

Historically, though, a sizeable majority of hikers have come from a white and upper- and middle-class demographic. Experts agree that we have a long way to go along the trail to equity in the great outdoors, and much increased efforts are necessary to welcome *everyone* into parks and onto pathways.

Accessibility is a major challenge. About 80 percent of Americans live in urban areas and typically those who live in lower income, disadvantaged communities are located the farthest from parks and trails, and are less likely to have transportation— private cars or public transit—to the start of a hike.

So let's hike with kids, *all* kids. There's no better way of growing the hiker population so that it better reflects the changing face of the population at large.

Hiking: Green Exercise at its Best

The term "Green Exercise" refers to physical activities that give participants the benefits of exercise and direct exposure to nature.

A growing body of green exercise research shows that interacting with nature while exercising can positively influence health and well-being, relieve stress, and promote concentration and clear thinking.

In other words, walking city streets is okay, but not as beneficial to mind-body-spirit as hiking through a park, greenbelt, or nature preserve.

Hikers, whether they know it or not—and I suspect most don't—are the chief practitioners of green exercise, also practiced by kayakers, surfers, and cross-country skiers. People of all ages, particularly kids, enjoy major benefits from green exercise.

Nature is often nearby—if you know where to look. Urban/suburban hikers benefit greatly from greenways and green space—land partly or completely covered with grass, trees or shrubs—and may include parks, preserves, woods and wetlands. (Great places to take a hike with kids—especially younger ones.) The many benefits of green space to our environment—and to those who hike through them—have been well documented.

More recently, researchers are calculating the benefits of "blue space"—defined as all the surface waters that offer recreation nearby. Blue spaces, such as lakes, ponds and rivers measurably reduce "heat stress"—not to mention reducing the stress of the kids and adults who stroll, saunter, or hike along their edges.

Hiking: The Best Green Exercise

Walking and hiking seem like the same kind of exercise, and you might think the two activities work the same kind of muscle groups; surprisingly, though, they're markedly different. Recent research shows how our hearts, muscles, and joints perform in distinct ways during a hike on a trail compared to what they do on a walk on a sidewalk.

No Nature Deficit Disorder here: Little kids learn big things when they experience the joys of nature, up–close and personal.

How Kids Benefit from Green Exercise

- **Sensory stimulation**—noting colors and sounds from nature's diversity, breathing fresh air, being exposed to weather, experiencing a sense of adventure, excitement, fun, enjoying an escape from pollution.

- **Activity**—learning physical skills, achieving challenging tasks, enjoying the energy of physical activities.

- **Natural and social connections**—being with friends and family, watching wildlife, stimulating spiritual feelings.

- **Escape from modern life**—having time to think and reflect/clear the head, getting away from pressures and stress, recharging batteries.

Hiking on uneven terrain requires the body to expend 28 percent more energy than walking over flat ground. Trails that go up, down and sideways require slight shifts in the way hikers' leg muscles lengthen or shorten while hiking and the frequent changing of position increases the total energy used during a hike.

Clearly it's better for kids to take a hike than walk to school.

Okay, maybe that's not the conclusion we should draw from these studies...

Nevertheless, it's clear that hiking requires different muscles than walking, and the result is strengthened muscles in our hips, knees, and ankles that we don't often use.

Hiking in nature may offer similar great benefits for the brain, which is getting its own exercise as it continuously evaluates and reevaluates the natural surroundings, and makes incremental adjustments for travel along an uneven trail.

Studies show time in nature reduces the mind's tendency to "ruminate," a term psychologists use to describe negative, self-absorbed patters of thought that been linked to anxiety and depression.

In short, there is mounting evidence that hiking in nature increases positive mood and decreases negative mood. For body and mind alike, a hike is hard to beat!

The Cure for "Nature Deficit Disorder"

Richard Louv, in his landmark book, *Last Child in the Woods*, writes movingly about how most kids have become completely out of tune with nature and how we adults allowed, perhaps unwittingly encouraged, it to happen. He refers to this as "Nature Deficit Disorder." Unfortunately, we all suffer from it in one degree or another in our speeded-up, high-tech indoor lifestyles.

Research suggests Americans of all ages, particularly children, are replacing outdoor activities with indoor ones. A study sponsored by The Nature Conservancy identified "videophilia" (love of video/TV) as a cause of obesity, poor social skills, various attention disorders, and poor academic performance. Rampant videophilia is replacing outdoor activities.

Fortunately humans, most particularly young ones, have an innate biophilia—that is to say, a built-in love of nature, however suppressed it is in these modern times. Recent research has demonstrated that time spent in nature improves the health of children, increases their ability to concentrate, and boosts their self-esteem, emotional well-being and leadership skills. Hiking in the countryside relieves symptoms of depression (while walking in a mall actually increases feelings of depression). Hiking has been found to benefit children with ADD (Attention Deficit Disorder).

The latest research shows that children that grow up near nature become happier, better adjusted adults than those that don't. A comprehensive nationwide study in Denmark revealed that "children who grew up with the lowest levels of green space had up to 55 percent higher risk of developing psychiatric disorders independent from the effects of other known risk factors."

According to the study, kids didn't have to live in the remote countryside or forest to enjoy the health benefits of nature—just reside within a reasonable drive of parklands, trails and urban green spaces and spend time in the natural world.

Researchers also found that the results were "dosage dependent"—the more time in childhood spent in green spaces the better the chances of becoming a mentally healthy adult.

We know from the experiences of just about every culture in the world that families more closely connected to nature tend to be healthier and happier. One happy trend in North America is the increasing number of active mom groups with a focus on hiking. These groups offer the opportunity to get babies and young children on the trail in a safe and supportive way, as well as socialization with like-minded newer parents.

Let's give a shout-out to Shanti Hodges who began Hike it Baby (hikeitbaby.com) as a meet-up group in her Utah community and evolved it into a movement. As a new mom, she invited other moms with babies and young children to hike local trails. The group rapidly expanded, and she is building a nationwide community of parents that shares hiking tips and kid-friendly trails.

Lately it seems that when the public discussion turns to school and how to improve student performance, the answer is technology. I agree up to a point. Technology has its time and place.

But these days, our children are more wired than their classrooms, enthusiastically embracing every device with a screen, while they seem more uncomfortable than ever in their own bodies in the real world. Teachers speak of digital whiz-kids who are clumsy and uncoordinated, even in performing the simplest of physical tasks.

It's time we get our high-tech kids some good old-fashioned outdoors time and space to think, feel and restore their souls in the real world beyond the computer lab, the classroom, the mall and the movie theatre. Politicians and government education officials often say: "We need to provide the latest technology and make sure every classroom is wired."

I say: "Kids don't need to be wired; they need to be walked: Walked in the mud and the rain and the heat and the cold. Walked in the forest and mountains, by the lakeshore and seashore. Kids should be walked until they're dirty and sweaty and tired—and happy, very happy—with their bodies exhausted, their souls stirred, and their minds and spirits renewed."

Hiking strengthens our most important relationships:
With family, friends, and the natural world.

2

Nurture

Years ago, I wrote a book about hiking *for* kids. It's a very upbeat book, with an emphasis on the fun kids can have in nature. My toughest editor turned out to be my then-10-year-old son. When Daniel read my first draft he was critical of my approach: "How come you keep telling kids hiking is fun. Kids know that, don't they?"

My young editor even got on me about offering basic hiking advice: "Kids know to stay on the trail and not cut switchbacks. Duh-uh!"

"Daniel, if I don't write about the fun of going hiking and I don't give kids tips on how to hike, what am I supposed to write about?"

"Just tell their teachers and their parents and the rangers to take them on a hike."

Can't argue with that logic.

Parents: You can do it!

Like most new parents, when our first child was a newborn, my wife and I were overwhelmed by the awesome responsibility—and some of the logistics—of caring for this new life. When we tucked our precious three-day-old daughter into a sling for her first walk outdoors, we considered our fears: What if the strap breaks, what if my wife trips and falls and crushes the baby; what if a dog jumps up and bites little Sophia, what if, what if, what if... .

Mind you, we're talking about a dad who's hiked all over the world and is in the business of telling other people to "Take a hike!" and about a mom who is a strong hiker and experienced outdoorswoman.

Believe me, I can relate to your fears.

Every parent can identify with those irrational thoughts, and every parent knows that no matter how old the child, those kinds of concerns never go away—as those once-tiny infants grow-up, drive, date and otherwise move to and through adulthood—all fraught with parental awareness about What Could Go Wrong.

We learned pretty early to do our best to keep both of our children safe—while at the same time provide them with the opportunity to gain rich learning experiences in nature. So we took them outdoors from Day One, scheduled family vacations in natural areas, and enrolled them in camps and schools that emphasized outdoor curriculum. And all those lessons may just have paid off.

When my daughter's ninth-grade class hiked up a steep mountain at the beginning of their autumn backpacking trip, her teachers reported about how she reached the peak, unloaded her pack, and headed back down the trail to help her friend who was struggling. She hefted her friend's pack and, together, they made it to the top.

That kind of story—what happens with your kids when you're not there—told me that all those hours on the trail made a difference in my daughter's trail savvy, and even more importantly, in her character.

Overcoming physical, mental or emotional challenges is part of life—on and off the trail.

"We used to go on hikes before the children were born…"

I've lost track of how many times parents have said those words to me—always with a deep sigh at the end.

Perhaps you feel the same way. How many adventurous singles became couples who shared time on snowy summits, explored remote canyons and partied hearty with their friends after a 10-mile hike? They thought that sense of freedom and exploration would last forever, but now—weighed down with family realities and responsibilities—it seems like a century ago.

When you have children, especially tiny ones, even the simplest hike can seem more daunting than organizing an expedition to the Himalayas. Thinking about packing all that gear, dealing with them on the trail, and keeping them happy afterward may sound too overwhelming to get out the door.

But don't hang up your hiking boots. Take your kids on a hike. And when you get them started young, everyone in the family gains valuable experience in taking to the trail, talking on the trail, and holding onto trail memories. The childhood years are fleeting, even if it seems impossible when you're holding an infant or the hand of a toddler, and contemplating taking that first step into the wilderness together.

Time on the trail and shared family experiences leads to improved communication and strong bonds that last a lifetime.

Be brave and confident, and embrace the hiking lifestyle with your children. Allow them to learn first-hand about the joys of nature and gain valuable life lessons in sharing, cooperation and personal accomplishment from their time on the trail.

Grandparents: Quality Time with Grandchildren

(Parents, read this and tell YOUR parents to take a hike—with your kids of course.)

Hiking is something you can do at most any age and stage of life. Grandparents who take an active role in introducing their grandkids to the great outdoors are heroes in my book. Apart from the physical challenges that come from, well, getting older, the wisdom that comes from age gives grandparents certain advantages in taking kids on a hike.

Grandparents can play a crucial role in getting kids on the trail, particularly in an era when parents are too busy to go hiking or disconnected from nature altogether. Older generations tend to be more comfortable in nature than younger ones and have more outdoor skills that they can teach kids.

Grandparents have the opportunity for real quality time with their grandchildren. On the trail and away from the distractions of modern life, the two generations are likely to have some great walks and talks. Kids will bring things up on the trail in conversation with their grandparents that they won't discuss back home with their parents.

Get started with a pack on your own back. Faster than you think, the grandkids will be walking and excited about their hikes with grandpa and grandma.

One of the fastest growing segments of the "Active Vacation" market is Grandparent-Grandchildren trips. Here's a typical pitch: "Share your love of the great outdoors with your grandchild(ren). Take short hikes together in the woods, swim in refreshing mountain lakes, then return to the comfort of our rustic lodge for..."

By all means, if you have the means, sign up for one of those grandparent-grandkid hiking holidays. But grandparents need not spend big or travel far to

Grandparents and grandchildren on the trail: Reconnect with nature and with each other.

take a hike. Find a state park or forest reserve nearby, inquire about the best trails for the grandkids in your charge, and off you go.

Make no mistake, taking a four-year-old on a hike is challenge enough for college-aged camp counselors and 20-something and 30-something parents, much less 60-something and 70-something grandparents. But with the right planning—and especially with the right positive attitude—it can be done, and done in a way that adds up to a joyful and memorable experience for grandkids and grandparents alike.

Youth Leaders: Special Tips for the Trail

Let's salute those caring adults (other than parents and relatives) who encourage kids along life's trails: youth pastors, Scout leaders, YMCA staffers, Boys & Girls Club crew and so many more.

A small number of these dedicated people have undergone formal outdoors education training and know how to teach hiking skills and present nature/science lessons. For most, though, taking kids on a hike is only a small part of their overall time working with youth. The big upside is that youth leaders who are good with kids often become excellent hike leaders after learning about hiking and spending time on the trail.

Youth leaders need not halt the hike in order to give "hiking lessons," but must be aware that the kids will be looking at you and up to you for guidance and as an example of a "good" hiker. Knowing that, have a proper standard of equipment.

Show up at the trailhead in hiking boots and seasonally appropriate outdoors wear. Take along a well-stocked day pack with an expanded first-aid kit, extra water and snacks.

Your main job as a hike leader is to establish effective communication with regard to the children's safety, comfort, and enjoyment and show by example how to move confidently when traveling along the trail. In other words, keep them safe and have some fun!

No need to flood kids with information about hiking technique and factoids about the environment. Instead go for "teachable moments" along the way. It will have been time well spent if kids have a fun time on the trail and a hike leader can communicate the following:

- Hiking can be a fun part of good physical fitness and staying healthy.

- Learning the basics of hiking will help you better enjoy this fun way to spend time outdoors.

- A hiker respects and cares for nature and the trails that lead to and through it..

- Time in nature is a way to gain peace, serenity and a different perspective.

Inclusion of Children With Disabilities

The importance of spending time in nature and getting time on the trail is incalculable, making access essential for everyone. Children with disabilities should be encouraged to enjoy the benefits of hiking, in whatever way it can work.

I've hiked with children on the autism spectrum, with children in wheelchairs, with children who are blind and with limited vision. All of these hikers delighted in their time on the trail, and got more out of their hiking experiences than I ever imagined possible.

Inclusion in the great outdoors is an attitude and approach that holds that every child, regardless of ability, can participate in nature-based activities. The good news is outdoors-oriented organizations are

Accessible pathways into nature offer wheelchair hikers independence and a fun, even triumphant, experience.

becoming more fully accessible to young people and meet-up–style groups (for moms and special needs children for example) are multiplying rapidly.

Wheelchair hikers are getting farther and farther from the trailhead with an assist from rugged, next generation off-road chairs with mountain bike tires. Thanks to our Digital Age, it's quick and easy to scout the accessibility of trails before venturing outdoors. Most parks—particularly federal and state ones, and increasingly at the local level, too—detail ADA-accessible trails on their websites and apps.

Whatever the difference, it can likely be accommodated, even with limited mobility or other challenges. It takes extra planning, knowledge about the challenges that might be experienced, a willingness to pick the right place and right pace, patience and a spirit of fun and adventure.

Don't overlook the National Parks and Federal Recreational Lands Pass (aka the America the Beautiful Access Pass), a free lifetime pass for U.S. citizens or permanent residents who have been medically determined to have a disability.

Disabilities are both visible and invisible. Kids are naturally curious when they witness what might be unfamiliar behaviors in other young hikers they encounter on the trail; most, though, are not judgmental and very accepting of differences, yet another lesson about hiking adults can learn from children.

Teachers: Lessons Planned and Unplanned

It's a challenge these days to take students out "just for a hike," however enjoyable and valuable that would be for kids. More than likely any school-sanctioned outing has a heavy science curriculum emphasis—often with homework, worksheets and even testing afterward!

My advice is to strive for a maximum of time on the trail and the least amount of time inside nature museums or listening to well-meaning park docents lecture about photosynthesis. Don't get me wrong; I fully support all studies in the natural sciences. Just know that it's more valuable and certainly more memorable for kids to splash in a creek than it is for them to study a diagram of the hydrologic cycle.

Nurturing a love of the great outdoors includes everyone, in all kinds of weather, like on this school-sponsored hiking adventure in Sequoia National Park.

Teachers may also take the time to research what great naturalists have written about the area, or what local writers have documented about the flora, fauna, history and other aspects of the natural world—and read to the group while on a rest break. Encourage students to respond with creative work of their own, in journals, sketchpads or notebooks.

Faith-based Youth Leaders: Fun and Fellowship

Many houses of worship sponsor hikes. I've been delighted to cross paths with many faith-based youth groups. The young hikers and their leaders represent a wide variety of denominations, ethnicities and economic circumstances.

Youth leaders most experienced with taking kids on hikes say don't wait for that week of church- or temple-sponsored summer camp to get kids into nature. Take them on a hike during the year! A hike offers fun and fellowship, with adults offering kids encouragement to grow spiritually and to contemplate their own existence and that of a higher power.

On the trail in the natural world, kids will often open up and talk to trusted adults in ways they wouldn't in the city or during the rush of daily life. Hiking with kids offers a great opportunity to support them during what might be difficult times in their lives.

Six Secrets to Hiking with Kids

- **It's the journey not the destination** Really, you don't have to get to the top of the mountain. It's about what you experience along the way.

- **Slow and easy** Don't push kids too long or too far, and make sure to take sufficient rest stops and snack breaks.

- **Say yes–yes–yes, not no–no–no** Be positive and avoid the don't-do-this-don't-do-that routine. Listen to them and be a little flexible about your time on the trail.

- **Teachable moments** When opportunities arise to impart some wisdom about hiking or the natural world, take advantage of the opportunity. Just remember you're not their science teacher.

- **Some challenge, please** A walk along a flat nature trail might be easy, but it's not a very exciting adventure. Kids like climbing boulders, running up and down hills, splashing in creeks.

- **Have fun** Forget about deadlines, heavy-duty responsibilities (besides keeping safe) and everyday stress, and let your inner child come out and play for the day.

A pack for every body! Day packs for kids and
adults come in a wide variety of sizes and colors.

3

Hiking Gear

Kids are likely to better connect with any sport or form of outdoor recreation if they are required to dress-up and gear-up to meet the challenges of the day. For hiking, it adds to the sense of anticipation and adventure if kids have a special cap, clothing, footwear and pack dedicated specifically for trail use.

If kids show up at the trailhead in the same clothes they wear to school or to the mall, such as cotton sweatshirts and skateboard shoes, they are less likely to consider the hiking experience special or show sufficient respect for nature, weather or the elements.

Importantly, though, the cost of gear should *not* be a barrier to hiking with kids. You can equip kids for the trail on a budget, even a very limited budget.

To get started hiking with children you don't need a whole lot of high-tech equipment—just the right stuff. The basics are a daypack, some good hiking boots, outdoors clothing and the Ten Essentials for everyone on the trail.

Tips for the Budget-Conscious

It's a great surprise to learn that so much specialty (read expensive) hiking apparel is available at thrift stores and secondhand consignment shops. It's a great, green lesson in reducing, recycling and re-using to purchase raingear and rugged outdoorswear—that still has plenty of wear in it for kids (and adults) equipping for the trail on a budget.

Moms and dads alike "wear" their infants, bonding in town and on the trail.

Among the items you can often purchase for about 10 to15 percent of original cost are fleece jackets and pullovers, zip-off pants, button-down shirts, water repellant outerwear (insulated and not) hats, gloves and nearly-new hiking boots. Especially keep an eye out for deals on quality child carriers (some originally costing $300).

Kids grow so fast that it can be a budget-buster and logistical challenge to keep replacing all their hiking clothes every year. Talk to your friends, neighbors and relatives. Ideally older kids pass along their outdoors clothing to younger kids. Put the word out on social media and don't be surprised if friends of friends come forward with offers of free kids' hiking apparel and gear.

All About Child Carriers

For good reason, hiking with a baby is often called "infant packing." When you gear up, the first decision is to choose a baby carrier. No, that's not a "who" question—as in "Who's the baby carrier you or your spouse?" Ha! It's really a "what" question—as in "What's the right baby carrier?"

The right carrier for an infant is a front sling or front pack. Babies need to be carried in front of us until about 6 months of age or so. When they've developed the neck strength to hold their heads up, they're ready to ride in backpack-style carriers.

You see a fair amount of front-pack style child carriers on the trail because they're popular in the city—particularly with so-called "baby-wearing" moms, those carrying a baby constantly. Models can carry 7 to 45 pounds, adjust to let the baby face outward, and have a removable/washable liner and sunshade. Colors and styles are many and varied—ranging from attention getting designer-edition prints to ultra rugged-looking front packs designed specifically for dads.

Slings, wraps and frameless carriers are fine, but hiking with an older, heavier child is so much easier when the weight is distributed with a framed hiking backpack.

Backpack-style Child Carriers

Leading backpack makers—including Osprey, Thule and Kelty—make child carriers and it's obvious that the same technical innovation that creates better and better backpacks with each passing year is also applied to improving child carriers.

If you are only going to use a child carrier for short day hikes or walks around town, opt for a basic model without all the accessories. Higher-end models have added options and, more importantly, better frames and suspension systems, which you'll appreciate on longer hikes and when your child gets older (heavier). Less expensive child carriers tend to have soft padding, supportive enough for short hikes, but the longer you're out—and the heavier the child—the less comfortable the carrier is for the wearer.

A good backpack-style carrier has a sturdy frame of light and tubular aluminum paired with a well-designed suspension so that the weight of the carrier and the child transfer away from neck and back and onto the hips, better to bear the weight.

A quality child carrier has easily adjustable padded straps and waist band, adjustable child harness, and a kickstand to keep the pack upright for safe loading and unloading of the child.

Top-of-the-line models come fully loaded with integrated sunshades that are quick and easy to deploy, plus plenty of covered pockets, mesh pockets,

A sturdy carrier, a strong parent, and a healthy sense of curiosity—add up to plenty of memorable experiences, wherever you hike with your kids.

and zippered hip band pockets. Some have a side entry option, which is useful for toddlers who can enter and exit on their own. Other options include a detachable diaper bag, detachable day pack, and a hydration reservoir (similar to and compatible with systems that integrate with day packs and backpacks).

Fitting the Child Carrier to the Adult

- First load carrier with heavy items (books for example) to approximate weight of child. Don't use an actual child while adjusting carrier.

- Adjust suspension system on torso so that the shoulder straps rest on shoulders and the hip band rests on hips (not on stomach or waist).

- Snugly tighten the hip band so that about 80 percent of the weight rests on your hips and tighten shoulder straps so that the remaining 20 percent of the weight rests on your shoulders.

- Tighten the straps (known as load-lifters) that extend from the top of the back panel to the top of the shoulder straps. If you spot a gap between your shoulder straps and the top of your shoulders, loosen the load-lifter straps and tighten again.

- Lastly, tighten the sternum strap across your chest but not so tightly that it constricts your breathing.

Fitting the Carrier to a Child

- Adjust the seat height so that the child's chin is even with the top of the chin pad.

- After making sure the kickstand is fully extended and the pack is stable, insert child through leg openings.

- Buckle and tighten straps. In particular, see that the shoulder straps fit evenly over the shoulder and leg straps are comfortable.

Carrier DOS & DON'TS

DO check on your child's neck support now and then; kids can fall asleep in the oddest of positions. DO periodically monitor body temperature and make sure your child is neither too hot nor too cold. DO clip a favorite toy to the carrier but perhaps not the *very* favorite because it might get jarred loose and lost or your little genius figures out how to unfasten it and drops it.

DON'T leave your child unattended in a carrier. DON'T place the carrier on an elevated surface such as a flat rock or picnic table. DON'T let the child eat (avoid any possibility of choking) in the carrier; instead, enjoy snacks at rest stops.

Day Pack Basics

A good day pack has a padded hip belt, padded shoulder straps, plenty of pockets and compartments, strong buckles and straps and covered zippers. School backpacks are fine for school and might do for a hike or two, but a pack specifically designed for hiking is the best way to go.

To encourage self-sufficiency and independence, even the smallest child should be encouraged to wear a tiny pack with a snack, and a small bottle of water inside. Keep the weight down to a bare minimum. As they grow stronger and more capable, provide better packs and have them carry their own extra clothing.

When packing a day pack, 1) Pack the heaviest items at the bottom, the lightest ones toward the top. 2) Pack items most likely to be used on the hike on top, so they're easily accessible. 3) Use pockets to keep water bottles and snacks easily accessible for hungry, thirsty little ones with little patience.

The best day packs are specifically designed for hiking.

Ten Features of a Good Day Pack

1. Durable weather-proof fabric

2. One-piece body construction

3. Padded shoulder straps

4. Padded back

5. Wide, padded lumbar belt

6. Sufficient pockets and compartments to suit your needs

7. Side pouch for water bottle

8. Strong buckles and straps

9. Storm flap-covered zippers

10. Strong top grab handle

Hiking Boots

The average adult hiker takes 2,000 steps to travel one mile of trail. Imagine how many steps a child must take to cover a mile?! So it's important to outfit kids with shoes and socks that keep their little feet comfortable and blister-free.

I admit my children wore hiking boots about as soon as they could walk and they were pretty darn cute. But they probably didn't need them. Sneakers will do just fine for toddlers, whose feet grow very quickly. Around the age of three or four, however, kids who really like to hike and can manage a mile or two, might especially enjoy the ritual of putting on their special hiking boots. School-aged children definitely should have hiking boots to protect their feet and stabilize their ankles.

Advances in hiking boots have brought us the wonderful lightweight models that resemble running shoes with a heavier sole. Make sure they fit with plenty of toe room for downhill hiking, and are wide enough for comfort. If the boots are a good fit, blisters are a thing of the past. Many hikers can wear new, lightweight hiking boots straight out of the box and onto the trail. If they feel a little stiff, though, break them in a bit before hitting the trail.

When you shop for hiking boots for kids, make sure they have room to wiggle your toes; the boots shouldn't be be so loose that they feel like they're floating in them. Tightness in the toe box can eventually lead to extreme discomfort later on, especially when hiking down steep down hills. Be certain their heels don't slide up and down when they walk, and stay put without feeling pinched. When boot shopping, have them wear the same type of socks worn on the trail. This helps ensure a good fit.

I will also admit that I'm a strict traditionalist when it comes to footwear on the trail; hiking sandals and toe shoes have their fans, but I'm lacing my boots and sticking with them, and recommending that you—and your kids—do the same.

Big and little: Hiking boots for the ages.

Hiking Socks

Socks made especially for hiking are more expensive than cotton athletic socks, but well-worth the investment to prevent blisters and keep feet dry on long hikes. These extra cushioned hiking socks absorb shock and provide comfort on the trail.

Wool is the most popular hiking sock material for good reason. It provides ample cushioning and regulates temperature well to keep feet from getting sweaty. Another benefit is that wool is naturally antimicrobial so wool socks retain smells less than synthetic fabrics. Okay, feet are still gonna smell after a long hike, but they're a lot less stinky coming out of wool socks.

Most socks are made of merino wool (much smoother and virtually itch-free compared to old school ragg wool socks) and are blended with synthetic materials for increased durability and faster drying.

Wise hikers pack an extra pair—and it's a good idea to change into them, since hiking in wet socks can be a soggy, miserable experience for kids and adults alike.

Clothing: Layering Made Easy

Dressing for a hike is as easy as 1-2-3. It's what hikers call "layering." Layering is just what it sounds like: if it's cold, rather than wearing one heavy coat, wear two or three thin layers. That way, if kids get too warm, they can remove any or all of the layers of clothing.

- A thin T-shirt made of a synthetic fabric will wick away sweat and keep skin dry, whether the weather is cold or hot.

- Over that, wear a button-down, long-sleeved synthetic shirt that can help control temperature by buttoning or unbuttoning, rolling up the sleeves, or keeping them buttoned.

- A good choice for the top layer is a fleece jacket or pullover, which looks great and keeps kids warm. It doesn't weigh much, and is easily stuffed into a pack, unlike a sweatshirt, for example, that is way too big and bulky for the trail.

Long pants are best in cold weather and some hikers like them in warm weather, too, because they protect against scratches and sunburn. Zip-off pants, long pants that have zippers above the knee, convert easily into shorts. (Keep track of the zip-off bottoms of convertible pants!) Shorts are fine—along with a liberal application of sunscreen, especially on tender calves and behind the knees.

Remember to bring a change of clothing for the kids. I confess I've forgotten extra clothes one too many times. You get 'em well outfitted for the trail, you take a fun hike and they get filthy and wet and...after the hike they have to ride home in soggy clothes and boy, do they let you know their strong feelings about this!

Rainwear

Hiking in the rain with kids might sound like an accident waiting to happen; without common sense and the right clothing, it could be. So play it safe and be smart whatever the weather, but especially under threatening skies.

Keep a lightweight rain jacket in the day pack for every member of the family, or hiking party. Stay away from vinyl, plastic or ponchos; opt instead for a quality jacket—at the very least made of coated nylon with its own little stuff sack.

A little bit of rain doesn't dampen the spirits of dedicated hikers.

Choose from waterproof models designed for seriously wet weather or breathable, wind-proof, water repellant rain jackets that shed light rain. Above all, keep those young hikers dry with the best outerwear you can find. Invest in higher quality outerwear and raingear when you see it on sale at your favorite outdoor retailer, or look for a bargain at a resale shop or garage sale. Those who live in wet climates, like the Pacific Northwest, will likely see the wisdom of investing in quality rain suits for everyone—or else spend far too many hiking days indoors.

The Ten Essentials

What must you always take on a hike? A Ten Essentials list was first shared among hikers in the

For younger hikers, consider the Cub Scout's "Six Essentials"—omitting, most notably, matches and the pocket knife.

1930s and is still used today. But on review, a few of the Ten Essentials are really items to help keep you safe if you should have to spend extra time—even overnight—on the trail. Avoid that circumstance at all costs, but, like a good scout, be prepared.

Some hiking experts count twelve or even fourteen essentials. And what about the daypack, essential to carry those essentials, shouldn't that count as an essential?

New hikers argue that a smartphone should be the eleventh essential while veterans insist it should be "common sense." Items that finish just out of the top ten but that are considered essential by some hikers include signaling devices (whistle, mirror) and insect repellant.

How many Ten Essentials are necessary for hiking with kids? Adults should carry all 10, while kids can carry fewer items. The Cub Scout "Six Essentials" list includes a safety whistle, which I wholeheartedly endorse as an essential for young hikers.

Most kids like to wear cool baseball caps and sunglasses. When they're old enough, get them a Swiss-Army knife—they're pretty light, even with a bunch of blades and a saw.

Kids really like headlamps and shining their lights at things; hopefully, though, they will have no need for illumination because adults will lead them back to the trailhead before dark.

Classic Ten Essentials

1. **Map** One that shows all the trails.

2. **Compass/GPS unit** Go hand-in-hand with the map; be advised: you're unlikely to get GPS readings (or cell phone reception) in remote places.

3. **Water** Bring plenty and drink before you're thirsty.

4. **Extra Food** Bring more than you think you might eat. Your hunger or day's plans might surprise you, and you'll want to be prepared.

5. **Extra Clothes** Pack rainwear and be ready for sudden changes in weather.

6. **First Aid Kit** And be sure to bring blister-treatment stuff, too.

7. **Pocket Knife** Very handy. Keep it clean and sharp. (Age-appropriate use only)

8. **Sun Protection** Sunglasses and sun screen with a high SPF made for kids.

9. **Flashlight/headlamp** You might have to hike after dark.

10. **Matches and Firestarter** Waterproof matches and something to get the flames going if you have to light an emergency fire. (Age appropriate use only)

Ten Essentials (Systems Approach)

To better meet the needs of the modern hiker, the venerable Ten Essentials list now referred to as the "classic" essentials has been revised and updated to what is known as a "Systems Approach," better reflecting modern outdoor recreation and all of the new

According to the latest edition of *Mountaineering: The Freedom of the Hills* book there are ten essentials, which are now referred to as the "classic" essentials. While still valid and widely used they do not reflect modern hiking and all of the new gadgets that now are common.

Individual items are now combined into systems. For example Map and Compass are now part of the Navigation System, along with the addition of GPS devices.

1. Navigation (map, GPS, and compass)
2. Sun protection (sunglasses and sunscreen)
3. Insulation (extra clothing)
4. Illumination (headlamp/flashlight)
5. First-aid supplies.
6. Fire (waterproof matches/lighter/candles)
7. Repair kit and tools.
8. Nutrition (extra food)
9. Hydration (extra water)
10. Emergency shelter

Other Items

- **Hat** to keep your body heat in, and the sun off your head. Baseball caps are a style choice and kids like to wear them. Wide brimmed hats are better for hikers but kids may resist them.

- **Insect Repellent** Keep those bugs away! But be aware that the American Academy of Pediatrics recommends the use of products with 10 percent or less concentration of DEET. Some parents may prefer to use products with natural ingredients only.

- **Trekking poles** Gives kids third and fourth "legs" on the trail. Trekking poles decrease fatigue while increasing speed and stability. Get poles that are collapsible, adjustable, and specifically designed for children.

Father and son: Matching caps, day packs, smiles. Happy Trails.

- **Bandana** Soak in water and wrap around neck to keep your cool on trail. Plus 100 more uses.

Energy To Burn: Favorite Trail Foods

It's okay to pack a basic lunch with sandwich, fruit and a cookie. Experienced hikers like to pack a variety of healthy and high-powered trail foods that can be eaten throughout the day. Snack often and enjoy the view.

- **Dried fruit** Easy to pack, it won't spoil or squish; a very tasty quick energy source.

- **Jerky** Plenty of protein and a cave man experience: the chance to gnaw away at dried meat in the middle of the wilderness.

Be sure to pack plenty of snacks to share with your trail companions.

- **Cheese and crackers** Hard cheeses pack much better than the softer ones.

- **Ants on a Log** Fill celery stalks with peanut butter and sprinkle with raisins.

- **Bars** Energy bars, granola bars, protein bars, sports bars, whatever you want to call them. Keep a few in your pack. If you don't eat them that day, they can keep for the next hike.

- **Chocolate** Tastes great at home, even better on the trail. Chocolate melts in the heat and turns into a gooey mess, but many kids think that it tastes better that way.

- **Trail Mix** Formerly known as GORP, for "Good Old Raisins and Peanuts," trail mix, has been a part of hiking for a way long time. But if trail mix only had raisins and peanuts it wouldn't be nearly as popular as it is today. Hikers have added all kinds of stuff to it over the years and everyone has their own favorite mix. Making your own trail mix at home—make it a project to share with the kids—is an easy and fun activity that allows you to throw together foods and flavors you really love: granola, M&Ms, carob chips, dried fruit (cranberries, apple, apricot, peach, mango, pineapple), banana chips, flaked coconut, shelled sunflower seeds.

Carrying Water

Water is the best drink of all—but, alas, do not drink water from any source on the trail except what you bring with you. You never know anymore what is upstream. Some hikers swear by so-called "energy" drinks or electrolyte replacements, but cool, clear water is just fine. With the environment in mind, avoid plastic bottles and choose a stainless steel reusable one instead. The half-liter size bottles are ideal for kids.

Considering some of the other stuff offered for sale in park gift shops and nature centers in popular hiking areas, a water bottle inscribed with a place name can be an excellent souvenir purchase for your kids. You could do a lot worse than a "Yosemite National Park" or "Appalachian Trail" water bottle.

Half–liter bottles are best for pint–sized hikers.

For more Tips about Gear, visit

TheTrailmaster.com

A hiker's dream: a single–track trail
(wide enough for only one person) meandering
through a field of wildflowers.

4

All About Trails

A good trail is like a good guide, pointing things out and picking the very best route from place to place. The best hiking trails don't go from point A to Point B in the fastest way, but take the scenic route. A good trail switchbacks (zigzags) up and down a mountainside rather than heads straight up it—but children don't usually appreciate the back-and-forth uphill climb. They sure like the downhill, though!

Most hikers don't think about who keeps the trails repaired, but in most cases it's the trail users themselves. Consider taking a family day to volunteer to work on a trail. It's hard digging and clearing brush but it feels really good knowing that you're keeping the trails open and doing something for your fellow hikers. There's a big National Trails Day in June, when hikers from all over America work on the trails.

How to Pick a Hike Kids will Like

What's a great trail for kids? The easy answer is one they'll enjoy. Elements contributing to a great hike for kids are unusual landforms, forests (ancient or at least mature), wildlife-watching and water in any form—streams, lakes, ocean shores. Kids also like panoramic views, solitude, cultural and historical sites, but often lack the same enthusiasm as adults for these aspects of the hiking experience.

Kids also like hikes that involve getting wet and/ or dirty. Swimming or just wading and splashing in water are high on the list of why kids like to hike.

Travel time to the trailhead must also figure into picking a hike kids will like. Ask yourself: How far out there do we want to get? How remote a trail do we want to hike? How far, how long do we want to travel to the trailhead?

Generally speaking, the younger the kids, the faster you want to get them out of the car and onto the trail. Some kids, though, travel really well and can handle longer car trips to the trailhead. For the younger ones, a short drive and a hike along a pretty little stream is usually a better bet than a long drive and a hike along the shore of an enormous lake.

Research the best hikes for kids online and by purchasing a trail guide to the area you want to hike. Take it from one who has written more than two dozen guides, the best guidebooks have basic accuracy of course, along with nature notes, colorful local histories and really evoke the spirit of a particular trail.

Online research is a good start. I recommend calling a park office or ranger station and asking a live human being about the best hikes for kids. Be sure to mention who's going hiking: the perfect family hike and the ideal trek for a large group of teens likely is not the same trail. You might be surprised and delighted to learn about a less-traveled trail or a scenic gem located off-the-beaten path.

While we're on the subject of choosing a great hike, I'm often asked by parents and youth leaders:

Pick a hike the kids will like and head for the trailhead.

Should we join a guided nature hike offered by this or that park agency or conservation organization?

My answer is a definitive...maybe.

First a shout-out to the many interpretive rangers, docents and volunteers who give of their time and of themselves to lead nature hikes. I've been on dozens of interpretive walks led by these dedicated souls. In my view, the hikes most enjoyable for kids are the ones with the most hiking and the least talking. Kids like learning fun factoids about nature but don't like to feel like they're in a classroom when they're on the trail.

My kids liked a few of the more entertaining ranger-led hikes in national parks but for the most

Nature hikes lead to other interests, like bird—watching, journaling and photography.

part got very antsy on guided walks around local historical parks and nature preserves. On the other hand, I've taken school groups on hikes and the volunteer docent who accompanied us on the trail added a great deal to a great day.

Easy and Hard Hikes: Trail Difficulty Ratings

Trails and hikes are typically rated (for adults) by their level of difficulty—usually Easy, Moderate or Difficult. For example, an Easy hike might be less than 5 miles with an elevation gain of less than 700 feet or so. A Moderate hike might be 5 to 10 miles with less than a 2,000-foot elevation gain. A Difficult hike might be more than 10 miles long with an elevation gain of more than 2,000 feet.

When planning a hike for the family, especially for little ones who need a positive introduction to the joy of hiking, plan in terms of minutes, not miles. A 30- to 45-minute hike is a long time for a toddler, though quality time on the trail can vary a great deal with a particular child's stamina, enthusiasm and attention span. End the hike on a high note with them wanting more, not whining that they're tired, bored and miserable. Banish any thoughts you might have to attempt a tough trail with a little kid—unless you want them to hate hiking—and the adult who took them.

Hikers can choose among many different kinds of trails. Often the best trails for kids are hikers-only paths (no other users permitted) and single-track (wide enough for only one person) trails.

Types of Trails

- **Nature trails** are short, usually interpreted trails that help you learn about plants, animals, history and the nearby environment.

- **Out-and-back trails** are those you use both coming and going.

- **Loop trails** are favorites of many hikers, because you circle around and see something different with every step along the way.

- **Multi-use trails** permit more than one group at a time (horseback riders, mountain bikers, hikers). Families with small children should use great caution on these trails. You don't want little hikers anywhere near mountain-bikers bombing down the trail.

Taking Care of the Trail

Trails are a special resource and hikers at an early age need to learn to take care of them. Tell the local land managers about trails that need repair. Poor design and weathering contribute to washouts and trail erosion, and so do hikers by overuse and poor trail sense. Hikers can best take care of the trail if they remember:

- **Travel in Single File** Most footpaths are made one-hiker wide and should not be widened by hikers who tromp on either side of the tread. Doubling up on a single-track trail is neither a safe nor an eco-friendly way to go.

- **Stay on the Trail** Staying on the trail is always a good idea but it's absolutely essential for protection of terrain such as bogs and alpine meadows. Also be sure to stay on the trail while hiking.

- **Never cut switchbacks** Repeat: Never cut switchbacks.

- **Muddy going** Kids have a primal attraction to mud and, if left to their own devices, will hike right through the middle of a muddy trail. Funny enough, so should all hikers! To best preserve the

No greater childhood joy than splashing through a mud puddle.

trail, hike through the mud rather than creating a new route that detours around mucky areas.

- **Trail Right of Way** Those triangular yield signs, with arrows going around a triangle from symbols of a hiker to a horse to bicycle mean "multi-use trail." The trail right-of-way rule is: hikers yield to equestrians, bicyclists yield to both equestrians and hikers.

Leave No Trace

"Leave No Trace." If you spend much time hiking or camping, more than likely you've heard the phrase and seen the popular logo on trail brochures, outdoor recreation websites, caps, T-shirts, you name it.

"Leave No Trace," refers to best practices for enjoying and protecting natural places. Learn more from the Leave No Trace Center for Outdoor Ethics (lnt.org), which promotes its principles, and leads service projects and educational programs across the U.S. and around the world.

Leave No Trace Principles

- Plan ahead and prepare.

- Travel and camp on durable surfaces.

- Dispose of waste properly.

- Leave what you find.

- Minimize campfire impacts (be careful with fire).

- Respect wildlife.

- Be considerate of other visitors.

Walk the walk, talk the talk

Share These Trail Words and Terms with Kids

Cairns Piles of stones that mark the trail. Also called "ducks."

Day hike A hike that begins and ends during daylight hours.

Degree of difficulty Measurement of how hard the hike is. Ratings include Easy, Moderate, Difficult.

Grade The amount of elevation change (steepness) between two points on the trail.

Elevation Measurement of altitude above sea level. The difficulty of a hiker goes along with how much elevation gain is required.

Hike To walk in nature.

Junction The point at which a trail meets another trail.

Loop trail A trail that completes a circle.

Nature trail A path with signs identifying plants and describing other natural features.

Pace The speed at which you walk or hike, often expressed in miles per hour.

Summit The top of a mountain

Switchback A zigzag, back and forth route up a mountain.

Trailhead Start of the trail.

A park ranger is a true natural resource,
a dependable source of information,
inspiration and trail smarts.

5

Hike Smart

Hiking on a trail is one of the safest activities you can do with kids as long as you hike smart—that is to say, plan well, know a few practicalities and outdoor recreation skills, obey human and natural laws, and use common sense.

Before you depart on a hiking trip with kids, share your itinerary with a friend or family member. Be sure to indicate when you expect to return; follow-up with your contact if your plans change.

Weather To Go

Get the latest weather report for the area where you'll be hiking. It's so easy to get an instant weather report on our digital devices, but be careful how you use the information because sometimes this data is for a nearby city and not indicative of the actual countryside that you intend to hike. Often a parkland, canyon, lakeshore, seashore, forest or mountain range will have an entirely different microclimate or weather pattern than the nearest population center. It's always wise to contact the nearest ranger office or park visitor center to double-check the weather forecast.

While I have been known to encourage grown-ups to take a hike in a light-to-medium rain, the best advice is to always err on the side of caution when little ones are involved. That being said, a short hike in the elements can be a memorable experience if precautions are taken, particularly on a well-signed trail that does not get muddy or slick.

Rain gear will make the hike more enjoyable when it's a simple shower or a drizzly day, but if there's any threat of really bad weather, or such dangers as flash

Ridin' in the rain, a great way to go.

floods, lightning storms, or worse, stay indoors and wait for more appropriate conditions.

If you decide to take a hike on a cold day, or in the snow, be sure to dress appropriately with gloves, hats, scarves and a warm jacket. On a hot day, you might want to just reschedule the hike, or wait until the weather cools; use your skills and the benefit of the latest forecast and always be weather-wise.

Help Kids Set the Right Pace

Dawdling down the trail, racing to the top of the mountain and every hiking speed in between are all fine ways to go. For safety's sake, though, it's important to know how fast you and kids hike (your pace).

The goal is to find a pace that's right for the kids in your charge. Know their limits, but also challenge them a bit. Adults hike 2 to 3 miles an hour. Kids hike about 1 to 2 miles an hour. Speed will vary depending on the difficulty of the trail. Adults are often surprised how far kids can hike, and kids surprise themselves, too!

Calculate in advance how long the hike will take, based on the pace of the slowest member of the group, and including lots of stops. Allow plenty of time to return to the trailhead before dark. On the trail, re-calculate based on the actual pace of the kids. Adjust—and turn around if necessary, because safety is the first priority.

Hiking speed, particularly for kids, is affected by the condition of the trail. Obviously a sprightly pace is easier to maintain on a smooth and wide trail than on a rocky and root-covered one, when it's necessary to look down at your feet just to stay upright.

Switchbacks are the hiker's friend. Some trails have few or none, others have sufficient switchbacks for steady, hiker-friendly ascents and descents. Young hikers will maintain a faster pace on a well-engineered pathway with plenty of switchbacks than on a straight-up-and-down route.

Grade is the amount of elevation change between two points on the trail in a given direction, and that sure affects your hiking speed. Kid-friendly trails have less than a 10 percent grade—or less than 500 feet of elevation gain over the course of a mile.

Onward and upward, at just the right pace.

Help Kids Learn to Hike in a Group

With larger groups of kids, the idea is to hike as a cohesive group while at the same time making sure each individual child has fun and a rewarding experience. Establish leadership roles before you start out. Designate a leader to stay in front, and appoint another adult to bring up the rear. A good rule is one adult per five to six children; keep the group in that order.

- **Agree on stopping points** Discuss in advance any trail junctions, scenic spots or other special resting places where the entire group will meet up.

- **Keep the group together** Insist on staying within sight and staying on the trail.

- **Avoid jailbreaks** Beware that at the trailhead or after a rest stop, kids, being kids, will take off running down the trail.

- **Count noses and institute a buddy system** Have the children choose a hiking buddy to care for each other and alert an adult in case of a problem; always count noses at each stopping point.

- **Encourage young hikers to be resourceful and responsible** Instruct them to think, be observant and pay attention to where they are going. Keep them on their toes and switch places in the line at stopping points.

Help Kids Develop a Sense of Direction

Almost all adults and kids navigate these days by roads, not footpaths, by the built world, not the natural one. Hiking offers the opportunity to re-connect with nature by paying attention to natural geography and navigating by way of rivers, mountains and valleys.

A hike is the perfect opportunity to help kids develop a sense of direction. Very few kids—and not many adults—know how to use a map and compass. A lost art, to be sure. Teaching kids to make use of modern navigation methods such as GPS is all well and good and, if it helps kids with their orientation in the great outdoors, we should encourage it.

Some kids, like some adults, have a great natural sense of direction. Other kids and adults, while lacking an innate sense of direction, can develop one by practice. A good sense of direction begins with paying attention to the geography around you.

When you and kids are on the trail, keep your eyes open. You'll get more out of the hiking experience *and keep from getting lost.*

STOP once in a while. Sniff wildflowers, splash your face in a spring. LISTEN. Maybe the trail is paralleling a stream. Listen to the sound of mountain water. On your left? Right? LOOK AROUND. Look up at that fire lookout on the nearby ridge. Are you heading toward it or away from it?

Staying Oriented and on the Trail

To stay oriented (and avoid getting lost!) encourage kids to:

- **Watch for waymarks** Pay attention to signs, mileage markers, disks, posts and piles of stones known as cairns or ducks.

- **Be aware of your surroundings** Note passing landmarks and distinct natural features en route such as unusual trees or rock formations. Compare your progress on the trail to the route on the map.

- **Think for yourself** Just because you're in the middle or at the end of the line of hikers doesn't mean you can stop thinking for yourself and stop paying attention to where you're going.

- **Have eyes in the back of your head** Look behind you to see what the land looks like from the other direction. Knowing where you came from always gives you a better feel for where you're going and prepares you for the return trip.

- **Follow the position of the sun** Use the east-rising, west-setting sun and its respective position on the trail to help you in your orientation.

- **Put the trail into words** Sharing what you see with a trail companion can help you stay oriented. Two heads are better than one, four eyes better than two, when it comes to staying on the trail.

Help Kids Watch For Wildlife

For kids, a memorable wildlife sighting can make a good hike great. Learn where the wild things are by consulting a regional guidebook, searching online, or asking staff at park visitor centers.

Don't think you need to find a moose with a sky-scraping set of antlers or other large mammal to wow the kids; they delight in watching pint-sized critters. Kids will while away half an hour playing peek-a-boo with pocket gopher popping its head above ground. If kids "only" see a rabbit, squirrel, frog, raccoon, duck, or covey of quail, they will be delighted, not disappointed.

I've led children on hikes who were hugely fascinated by watching a banana slug move across a trail. Much to my impatience, the kids wouldn't budge until the slug crawled sluggishly away.

Better than Bambi: The sight of real deer in the wild.

Most wildlife checklists obtained from park offices are big on birds. While flying or roosting, birds are often easy to spot—at least easier than most quadruped-type animals.

Many kids are fascinated with winged creatures. Often there are bird species aplenty in every ecosystem and near many a trail: resident songsters, waterfowl, migrants from near and far.

Wildlife-Watching Tips

- Animals are particularly active in the early morning and late afternoon.

- Hike slowly, hike quietly.

- Keep your distance. Never purposely scatter birds or butterflies to get them to take flight or give chase to an animal.

- Binoculars or a spotting scope help deliver close-up views.

- Look for signs: tracks, scat, bedding sites, burrows, mounds, cavities.

- Stay on maintained trails. Animals often take the easiest and direct path through the woods—just like hikers!

- Don't feed wildlife. Nature provides adequately without supplemental feeding from humans. Let the kids know our human food can be harmful to animals.

Life Lessons on the Trail

Pay attention to the mood, the feel, the commentary and the natural ease among your hiking group. It may be the time for a teachable moment or even a deep conversation.

It's less about what you say, though, and more about what you do. Kids will pick up on your positive example. If you're a hiker role model, kids who are stronger hikers will follow that model and begin helping those having a harder time on the trail.

Part of learning to hike is learning to work and play with others. You certainly don't want to halt kids on the trail and make a big deal to kids out of the potential life lessons of hiking. But character counts on the great trail of life and there are four, easy-to-share, age-appropriate life lessons that you can share with kids:

- **Hikers work as a team** Offer comfort to the younger hikers if they're slow, tired or don't feel well. Use kindness and encourage them with positive words. Help them out by carrying some of their things in your pack, or by offering water or a little snack.

- **Hikers do unto others** Think about how you would want to be treated on a hike and treat your fellow hikers that way.

- **Hikers don't whine** There's no whining in hiking. Make sure this is enforced! Whining can be contagious among kids. You (and the kids themselves) know how awful it is to be around someone who whines, so head it off: Offer a snack or a drink; provide a change of pace by slowing down or speeding up; offer distractions with the view, storytelling, anything to keep the whiners otherwise occupied.

- **Hikers have an attitude of gratitude** Always remember that the natural world is the one in which we're meant to live. It's beautiful, free and fun. How thankful we should be for a day outdoors and our many freedoms. Count your blessings and vow to hike again soon.

For children, hiking offers a lot of fun, and a few life lessons, valuable on—and off—the trail.

After the Hike: Share the Experience

Walk the walk and talk the talk.

If you are comfortable doing so, share trail accounts and meaningful moments with your circle of friends and community at large. Every time you mention a hike with kids in conversation or share stories and image on social media you help spread the good word. If you are media savvy and feel motivated to do so, consider share your hiking experiences with the media platforms of parks, regional travel bureaus, conservation organizations, community organizations and newspapers...you might be surprised to learn who's interested in your tales of happy trails!

Having said that, let me quickly add that I'm rather conservative about posting anything, even hiking-themed images, about the children in my life. If like me you have concerns (data mining, creepy strangers having access to photos of kids, etc.) about images lingering on a worldwide digital platform in perpetuity, then carefully limit what you share—or don't share at all.

Experts say that at around 5 years old children start to develop a sense of themselves as individuals and it starts mattering to them how the rest of the world perceives them. Their privacy should be of concern to us.

It's likely a majority of kids, though, would rather have attention than privacy. Kids readily, often instantly, share hiking adventures with their peers. Kids being kids, don't be surprised if that short hike they didn't seem to like all that much turns into a fun, epic adventure when they share photos and video.

Get more Tips about how to "Hike Smart" at

TheTrailmaster.com

When should you take kids on their first hike?
The sooner the better!

6

Hiking Through the Ages

From infants through teenagers, I've observed no single "right" or "wrong" age to take children on a hike. On a practical basis, each age of childhood offers both pluses and minuses; on a spiritual basis, the pluses prevail by far. Each age group presents different challenges and offers different opportunities to share the experience of hiking.

- **Infants** Practically speaking, infants are highly portable, but they require packing all this "baby stuff" to go along with them. Often they sleep a lot, but they can cry a lot when hungry, uncomfortable, or bored.

- **Toddlers** toddle, meander and bolt—but only occasionally in the desired direction.

- **Grade-schoolers** take a vigorous interest in hikes—but it might not be the same vigorous interest as their parents.

- **Teens** can hike long distances, keenly appreciate both cultural sites and the natural world—but they often don't want to take such hikes with their parents—or for that matter any adult authority figure!

I'm very pleased that my own children learned, at an early age, to enjoy hiking—though some would point out they had little choice! Nevertheless, I learned early on what a privilege it is to share the joy of time on the trail with the little ones. Some of the most important lessons I've learned while hiking with my kids came to me when I stepped out of my role as parent and gave them a chance to lead me on their path.

Bringing Babies

From the moment a newborn joins the family, we anticipate, we celebrate, a child's "firsts": first smile, first laugh, first word, first steps… For parents who like to hike, another great moment awaits: baby's first hike!

There is something so natural, so primal about bringing a babe into the woods. Surely it deepens the bond between parent and child, and early exposure to the natural world might just prove to have long-lasting benefits for the youngest among us. And it's not just babies who benefit. Parenting a newborn can be a stressful undertaking; hiking in the fresh air is a good way for parents to get refreshed.

In my experience, babies, fed and comfortable, are great trail companions. Portable, easily amused, prone to napping in the fresh air, they're delightful, and delighted. It can be a meaningful hiking experience, a wonderful blend of nature and nurture.

When's the best time to take that first hike with baby? I say the sooner the better!

The old-fashioned sling helps new moms share time on the trail with their babies, special time together.

Tips for Hiking with Babies

- Begin with short hikes, a couple hours max; gradually add more miles and time on the trail.

- Babies aren't able to regulate body temperature like adults so be extra attentive when hiking in heat, cold, wind and rain.

- Protect your baby with a broad-brimmed sunhat, one that covers the neck.

- Make sure you—and your precious cargo—are comfortable with the carrier before you start your first hike.

- The hiking motion—the slight sway, the rhythm of walking—tends to put most babies to sleep, so consider scheduling family hikes at naptime to stay in synch with your baby's sleep cycle.

- Pack plenty of diapers as well as sealable waste bags to carry out the soiled ones.

- Avoid hiking at high altitude. Babies, particularly those who live with flatlander parents, do not adjust well to increased ear pressures and other strains of high altitude.

- Take it slow and easy. Don't try to ford fast-moving rivers or descend steep grades with that bundle of joy on your back. And always watch for low-hanging branches!

Trekking with Toddlers

This age group (from about 18 months to four years old) is all about the journey, and no idea of the destination; all about energy, exuberance, and gaining independence, without a clue about consequences.

When my son was a toddler, he liked to bolt from the trailhead like a racehorse from the starting gate. One time we started a hike at 9,000 feet elevation and he raced off across an alpine meadow, soon running out of breath. And he cried, panting, "What happened?" Another time he exuberantly sprinted downhill as fast as his little legs would carry him and shouted: "This hill is making me run!"

Provide outdoor opportunities with proper boundaries that allow them maximum exploration and minimum frustration. Since toddlers often wander into the land of "no," it's important to make hiking a place of "yes," as much as possible. The art of hiking with toddlers, then, is to be patient and let them enjoy the journey—you will too.

Tips for Hiking with Toddlers

- **Stay away from scary** The easiest hikes for toddlers are those where they can wander and run—and parents know they will be safe. Save those cliffside adventures, boulder-hopping stream crossings and cross-country trail-less adventures for when they're steadier on their feet and more responsive to warnings of danger.

- **Open space rules** Think instead about taking toddlers to experience nature in wide meadows, easy nature trails and gentle beaches, where they can run as fast as their little legs can carry them, and enjoy the great sense of freedom and open space they long for—without endangering themselves or being scolded for heeding their inner nature.

- **Small is beautiful** The flip side of the desire to run wild is that slowed-down tiny observation of

Hiking with toddlers often means sitting with toddlers while they explore nature at their feet. Remember to be patient and enjoy the moment.

the world according to a toddler—that may seem like stubbornness to an adult, but it very meaningful to the child. My daughter, for example, loved Peter Rabbit books, stories and characters—every one of them. And every time we went anywhere near a forested area, all she wanted to do was to get as close to a big gnarly tree or hollow log as possible, and act out those favorite stories that she had stored in her imagination and that simply came alive to her in the natural world.

- **Take your time** While sometimes difficult, do your best to allow kids to enjoy the woods in the way they want—and adjust expectations and schedules accordingly. The huge trees in an old-growth forest that you want to show a child may not be nearly as interesting as a burned-out portion of a tree that offers a marvelous little "house" to play in.

Hiking with School-aged Kids

It's the Golden Age of Hiking with Kids— from about 5 to 12—when children are typically inquisitive, enthusiastic, and joyful about new experiences and learning about the world around them. By 5, kids can stay out for several hours and hike a few miles. Enjoy this opportunity to instill appreciation for nature, and take them hiking as often as possible. The experience will enhance your relationship and deepen your connection with your kids—and theirs with the natural world.

Tips for Hiking with School-aged Kids

- **Keep children in sight at all times** Tell them they have to be able to see you. That may seem obvious, but you'd be surprised how fast kids can get off the trail.

- **Repetition counts** Keep it fun, but repeat and repeat again all instructions ranging from snack breaks to port-a-potty locations.

- **Choose a hike with modest elevation gains** Children prefer intimate settings, such as a little creek or a clump of boulders to those vast scenic panoramas favored by adults.

- **Feed the troops** Begin with a nourishing breakfast. Carry plenty of quick-energy snack foods

Hiking with school–age kids: more miles, and usually, more smiles.

and offer them frequently. (Don't wait for the whining: By the time kids tell you they're hungry, they're often already cranky and out of both energy and enthusiasm.)

- **Supplement the Ten Essentials** Bring extra snack foods, whistles (in case you and your child become separated), a book or toy for the drive to and from the trailhead.

- **Check temperature** While you'd think that kids would tell you if they're too cold or too hot, they often don't. Dress them in layers and be sure to add or subtract clothing in response to changing weather conditions.

- **Teach respect for nature** Enjoy but don't disturb flowers, plants and animals. Environmental education is easy and fun on the trail, so be sure to pack a good trail guide or nature guidebook and visit park interpretive centers.

- **Bring a friend** When children travel in groups, the kids motivate each other to go farther and faster. And there's a lot less complaining.

- **Take it easy** It's much better for everyone to stop frequently and travel slowly than to try to make the kids go faster and then have to carry them. If parents know what kids can and can't do, everyone has a great time on the trail.

Hiking Games

One-Two-Three-Jump With an adult holding each hand, the child hikes along one-two-three steps, then jumps as parents raise arms and swing the hopefully-no-longer reluctant little hiker into the air.

Would you rather? Take turns asking "Would you rather....?" questions. When you're out hiking, nature oriented questions are particularly fun: ....be invisible or able to fly? ...have 3 legs or 3 arms? ..kiss a frog or hug a snake? ...be able to control the weather or talk to animals?

I Spy is another favorite trail game: "I spy with my little eye something that is....(fill in the blank). Variations include, "I smell with my little nose," and "I hear with my little ear."

Hiking Hide and Seek (play this game with older kids who won't venture so far off the trail that they get lost!) The designated hider runs ahead on the trail and finds a place (rock, tree, whatever) to hide behind or under—10 to 20 feet from the trail is about right. Everyone else keeps hiking at normal pace and (hopefully) located the hider. Alternate hiders so that everyone—children and adults—gets a chance.

Scavenger Hunt Print out one of those colorful lists from Pinterest or pick a half dozen or so items to locate before going on your hike. Go with a traditional approach (something blue, something human made, an animal's home, a rock shaped like a heart, three different shades of green…) or orient your list to the particular area where you're hiking. Observe all park rules pertaining to the collecton of natural objects.

Hike-ku A haiku is a poem that has three lines composed of five syllables, seven syllables, and five syllables. They're fun to compose while you're on the trail. I call them hike-kus.

Here are a few my kids and I composed on the trail:

We hike all morning
And finally reach the top
Joyous mountain high

Rubbing the wrong way
my new boots look wonderful
Blisters temper joy

Trail mix by handful
healthy nuts and raisin crunch
eat M and Ms first

Hiking with Teens

As with every age group, adjust your expectations to the developmental stage of the child. Don't be surprised when your 12-year-old suddenly is more interested in going to the mall with friends than taking a hike with you. But this is the time of parenting when the art of compromise, negotiation—and sometimes gritting your teeth—comes into play.

Truly, teens can be the most challenging of trail companions. They're too young (in most circumstances) to hike on their own and they're reluctant to hang with their parents, even surrounded by stunning wonders of nature. And oh, the attitude!

Ah, but there's something about hiking on the trail and being out in nature that may make this age group more willing to talk about important matters than any other place. Give it a try.

Encourage older, more independent teens to get out on the trail with their friends as a healthy, lifelong path to fitness, managing stress and setting goals—and achieving them.

Tips for Hiking with Teens

- **Attitude is everything** Be aware that teens are prone to BAS (Bad Attitude Syndrome). More than any other age group, they're apt to be lazy, sullen, grouchy or downright mean on the trail, and express their contrariness in No Uncertain Terms. Realizing this, do your part to lighten up and have fun.

- **Friends** Teens are human, too (really) and there's nothing like a hike to diminish BAS. In their own way, and in their own time, this age group does find joy in hiking, especially if they're allowed to Bring A Friend—the main goal at this age. Parents: Allow a friend to accompany you, particularly if it's a spunky kid with a good attitude

- **Clothing** Let 'em wear cool clothes. Provided teens dress in layers with the proper kinds of apparel, let them have input about colors and styles—but draw the line at safety issues or anything that

With teens, attitude—yours and theirs—is everything when it comes to having happy trails.

involves a discussion of skinny jeans, flip-flops, and tiny tank tops. Use the art of compromise here—running shoes are a reasonable substitute for boots for all but the most rugged hikes.

- **Tripping** Involve them in the trip-planning and they'll be happier hikers. Ask for their input about the hike's distance and destination, about where to stop for a dinner on the drive home.

- **The hike** Choose hiking activities with some excitement. A swimming hole or a waterfall is a more appealing destination than a historic grist mill.

- **Enhancing the relationship** Use the time on the trail to talk—and really listen. Teens are often able, and willing, to express what's on their minds while on a hike.

- **Challenge them** Adults are often more surprised than the teens themselves at the mountains they can climb and the distance they can cover.

- **Be here now** Take a hike and take a digital day off. Stay in the moment and off the phone.

- **Give them space** A little separation at carefully selected times/places is okay. Let them hike a little ahead of the adults—provided there's a well-understood agreement to meet at a particular time or place.

- **Packing** Encourage them to wear their daypacks correctly (which they probably don't do with their school backpacks). Insist they adjust the shoulder straps and fasten the hip band.

Take a ~~Walk~~ Hike Near Home

You might be surprised what a little research might uncover in the way of greenery and scenery near home. Here's how you can turn a walk into a hike kids will like:

- **A walk in the park** Away from traffic, city and suburban parks are islands of greenery and nature.

- **Meander down by the riverside** The sound of running water is particularly restful to us. De-stress by walking alongside a river.

- **Make tracks** Rails-to-Trails Conservancy, along with governmental agencies, has converted thousands of miles of out-of-use railroad tracks to trails. Check out railstotrails.org to find a trail near you.

- **Walk with the animals** Nearby wildlife refuges, estuaries and bird-watching sites often have trails leading to, or around them. A "Zoo Hike" is always a hit with kids.

- **Walk U** College campuses offer safe walkways, fitness trails, even gardens and nature paths.

- **Busman's holiday** Take a bus to the edge of the city and walk back or walk to the end of the bus line and bus back.

Bringing the Family Dog

For some families, heading out for a hike would be unthinkable—and no fun at all—if the family dog had to stay behind. But much as you love your pet, know that dogs are not welcome in many parklands and nature preserves, as well as on many trails. Contact park or forest offices and find out the rules and regulations for dogs on the trail.

Many dogs love to take a hike and love the "quality time" with their owners. And kids love hiking along with the family dog. Make sure, though, you make a candid assessment of your dog's energy level and condition. Not every good dog is a good hiker.

Paws on the trail: Dogs can be great companions on a family hike.

Tips for Hiking With Dogs

- Make sure your dog has up-to-date vaccinations and current identification tags.

- Only hike where dogs are allowed.

- Help your dog out with some flea and tick repellant.

- Bring water and a collapsible bowl. Dogs can get dehydrated and overheated, just like humans.

- Heed leash laws.

- Don't allow your dog to chase squirrels, deer or other wildlife.

- Clean up after your dog. If your dog brings it into the park, you need to hike it out. Use zippered plastic bags for disposal of waste. If you are far from the trailhead, bury dog poop in a "cathole," well off the trail.

- You and your dog must yield to all other trail users including cyclists and equestrians. Leash up and allow other trail users to pass.

- After the hike, check your dog for ticks and foxtails.

"Walk as children of light."

7

What Adults Can Learn from Kids about Hiking

Just as children enhance the lives of adults in myriad ways, children enrich any hike with their own special thoughts, feelings, and sensory impressions. They bring innocence, wide-eyed wonder and enthusiasm that knows no bounds on a hike. Their small steps are accompanied by great leaps in imagination.

Perhaps the most important words of advice I can offer on this subject are summed up in the very simple phrase, "Carpe diem." Seize the day, the moment, the opportunity to take your child into the great outdoors to experience the wonder, the magic and the gift of nature.

Childhood passes so quickly these days, with children and parents on an endless loop of mastery, achievement and performance of tasks that often have little intrinsic meaning, and don't resonate at all with the soul. Steal the time, if you have to, to get out and play.

I will confess that there have been times when I have decided that taking off a few days for hiking with my son in Yosemite was more important than state standardized testing. (Note to parents: Should you be similarly inspired to allow your child to take a hike rather than take a test, don't tell any school officials where you got the idea.) Guaranteed, that time in nature with his dad was more valuable to my son's education than any standardized test.

Walk as Children of Light

When she was a little tyke, one of my daughter's favorite books was *The Listening Walk* by Paul Showers. A little girl likes to take what she calls "listening walks" with her dad and notes the *thhhhhh* of a sprinkler, the *bomp-bomp-bomp* of a dribbling basketball, the *creet-creet-creet* of the crickets in the grass. "I hear all sorts of sounds on a listening walk," she says. "I listen to sounds I never listened to before."

Another favorite children's book, *Funny Walks* by Judy Hindley, opens with a question rarely considered by adults but perhaps often pondered by children: "Isn't it funny how people walk?"

One of the senses better developed in children than in adults is the sense of the ridiculous. What is a child to make of a walker with a scowl and a head bent down or one with a "thinking face" and hands in pockets? And isn't it odd how animals walk when you take the time to stop and watch?

"Walk as children of light," advises St. Paul, the Apostle. I've discovered that hiking with children has helped me become a better hiker—more adaptive, more sensory and more patient. On hikes near home or faraway, children are great conversation starters with strangers—particularly those with children of their own. Young hikers remind us that many of the world's most compelling sights are all around us, just waiting to be discovered.

With children, it's not how many miles you hike, it's how many smiles you share.

The Trailmaster's Ten–Point Plan for Getting Kids Back on the Nature Trail

1. Leave no child inside. Connect children of all abilities with nature.

2. Encourage both unstructured outdoor play opportunities and structured outdoor recreation programs.

3. Teach kids hiking, outdoors and life skills and, in so doing, enhance student performance and leadership abilities.

4. Promote hiking for good health—for physical, mental, and spiritual wellbeing.

5. Encourage good diet choices and regular green exercise.

6. Emphasize hiking in nature near home—the use of city parks, open space preserves and greenways.

7. Connect urban and ethnically diverse populations to the hiking experience and the great outdoors.

8. Expand hiking and outdoor recreation opportunities for families and help them create outdoor traditions.

9. Support parents with positive reinforcement and useful information about hiking, allay any fears and dispel any myths, and help them hike with their kids.

10. Help kids develop a sense of stewardship for the public lands and natural resources that they will eventually manage for themselves and the next generation.

HIKE ON.

Photo Credits

Michael Blum, p.98; Alberto Casetta, p. 54; Jank Ferlic, p. 96; Cindie Hansen, p. 84; Jens Johnsson, p. 78; National Park Service, p. 76; Kyle Nieber, p. 93; Derek Owens, p. 42; Kelly Sikkema, p. 71; James Wheeler, p. 16; Jamie Street, p. 105; Chen Zo, p. 22. Additional thanks to Unsplash and The Trailmaster Inc.

John's Books for children

JOHN MCKINNEY

John McKinney is an award-winning writer, public speaker, and author of 30 hiking-themed books: inspiring narratives, top-selling guides, books for children.

John is particularly passionate about sharing the stories of California trails and is the only one to have visited—and written about—all 280 California State Parks. John tells the story of his epic hike along the entire California coast in the critically acclaimed *Hiking on the Edge: Dreams, Schemes and 1600 Miles on the California Coastal Trail.*

For 18 years, he wrote a weekly hiking column for the *Los Angeles Times,* and has hiked and enthusiastically told the story of more than 10 thousand miles of trail across America and around the world. His "Every Trail Tells a Story" series of guides highlights the very best hikes in California.

The intrepid Eagle Scout has written more than a thousand stories and opinion pieces about hiking, parklands, and our relationship with nature. John's books for kids include *Let's Go Hiking* and *Let's Go Geocaching* and has long focused on inspiring a diversity of young people to hit the trail.

A passionate advocate for hiking and our need to reconnect with nature, John is a frequent public speaker, and share his tales on radio, on video, and online.

JOHN MCKINNEY:
"EVERY TRAIL TELLS A STORY."

HIKE ON.

TheTrailmaster.com